Author of One More Unfortunate

Eurydice, Ahoy!

A short account of a yacht cruise on Lake Champlain, in the summer of

1880

Author of One More Unfortunate

Eurydice, Ahoy!
A short account of a yacht cruise on Lake Champlain, in the summer of 1880

ISBN/EAN: 9783337410155

Printed in Europe, USA, Canada, Australia, Japan

Cover: Foto ©Andreas Hilbeck / pixelio.de

More available books at **www.hansebooks.com**

EURYDICE, AHOY!

A SHORT ACCOUNT OF A

YACHT CRUISE

ON

LAKE CHAMPLAIN,

IN THE SUMMER OF 1880.

BY THE AUTHOR OF

"ONE MORE UNFORTUNATE."

MONTREAL :
PRINTED FOR THE AUTHOR BY JOHN LOVELL & SON.
1881.

INTRODUCTION.

In the following pages, you, indulgent Reader, will find a "round, unvarnished tale"—a sketch, in short, taken from the log of the Eurydice, of a summer's cruise on American waters in a five-ton sloop yacht. It might be somewhat difficult, I am modest enough to remark, to find anything in particular to recommend this yarn to the public taste or criticism. In explanation of the above observation it may as well be stated honestly, so as not to mislead any lover of sudden death stories in yellow covers, that the yacht performed no such remarkable feat as foundering, and then appearing on the surface again ; or dashing through gigantic waves and, like a duck, shaking herself on the other side ; nor yet did she take a fancy to lie on her beam-ends as if to tumble out the ballast, both alive and dead.

Then again the crew, composed of owner, friend and small boy, were not responsible for any glaring eccentricity ; nor did they possess any particular virtue of character beyond that of endeavoring to remain upon the yacht under all circumstances, while sailing or at anchor.

The principal object of my book is to amuse if possible, personal friends, and to afford to the writer the pleasure of reviewing in his mind the incidents and scenes of what was to him a very happy cruise.

Another object to which this little book may lend its aid is that of creating and renewing the love for one of the manliest sports and pastimes ever indulged in ; judgment, nerve, and what is called pluck, are all brought into active exercise constantly. And what, may I ask, can possibly constitute a better discipline for man than that which makes him a man, in every sense of the word ?

> " Oh ! who can tell ? not thou, luxurious slave !
> Whose soul would sicken o'er the heaving wave ;
> Not thou, vain lord of wantonness and ease,
> Whom slumber soothes not, pleasures cannot please.
> Oh ! who can tell, save he whose heart hath tried,
> And danced in triumph o'er the waters wide."

Yachting ought certainly to be encouraged : no man can ever truly regret going in for it, thoroughly and scientifically. It is healthful, it is harmless, in so far as temptations to betting and the various vices and trickeries of the turf are concerned. Yachting men, as a rule, do not bet on the issues of races in regattas, or, if they do, not heavily as in horse races. There is no fetid atmosphere of corruption, no smells, no dust, no drunkards reeling about in connection with yachting; the air into which the tall tapering masts of the various yachts extend is as pure as the breath of heaven, the water is as clear as crystal.

Think, and you will find many more advantages which the one has over the other,—yachting over horse-racing—yachting over everything.

EURYDICE, AHOY!

CHAPTER I.

THE START.

THE preparations were somewhat hastily made, for we were most anxious not to lose time in getting afloat. Summer was rapidly passing into autumn, and the golden days were growing shorter. We met to compare notes with regard to what we were to bring with us. Our kit, roughly speaking, was composed of the following: one or two blankets, one railway rug (most indispensable article both on shore and aboard ship), a pillow each, and two changes of flannels, with perhaps a linen shirt, smuggled in by way of the possible contingency of being asked into polite society; then the provisions need not be enumerated, on the principle of—what you like, I like.

A beautiful cedar skiff, light and seaworthy, to be used as dingy, was pulled alongside, and the operation of transporting the cargo on board was vigorously begun. Then the stowing away, and examining the hold to see that no more water than was allowable was being made; the unfurling of sails and inspection of standing rigging and running gear and ballast was looked to. When all was ready the skipper gave the order to stand by the mainsail halyards, and helped to slip her moorings and hoist the jib. Our colors (my Cambridge Boat Club colors and the Dominion Ensign) floated at her mast-head as we proudly, and I may say gracefully, glided away on the port tack towards the open river and mid-stream channel.

The Commodore of the Montreal Yacht Club started about ten minutes after us in his steam yacht, his destination being the Richelieu near Lake Champlain. As we had a fair breeze he did not gain on us very perceptibly : an elongated island, causing a narrow inside channel, finally intervened between us—he having taken that course.

We had not taken a pilot on board, consequently a sharp look-out had naturally to be kept for the channel ; for in some places it is only three hundred yards wide ; there are two, the North and South. We took the South. Buoys to mark the channel, are placed at certain distances apart : as we passed one set, the field-glass was resorted to, to find the others. Then again there are also light-houses to steer by.

The scenery is pretty, but not striking, as there are no craggy bluffs or highlands, to strike and arrest the eye as one glides down this mighty tributary to the sea. We passed villages, plainly

characterized, as they are all over the province, by
their size and glittering appearance, caused by the
sun striking upon spires and tinned roofs.

When we had reached the broad part of the
river, about half way between Montreal and Sorel,
we hoisted the top-sail, which materially increased
our speed, and enabled us to run off about seven
knots, exclusive of current, which at that part of
the river might be put down at three miles an
hour.

The reader cannot adequately imagine, without experiencing it, the utter abandonment to
pleasure the scene and circumstance afforded—the
motion of the yacht dancing from wave to wave,
with the white foam sportively playing about her
bow ; the sense of freedom from restraint and
comfort in looking into our snug cabin where,
safely deposited, was all that contributed to our
material wants, not omitting the fragrant weed.
When we had passed this lake, as it might be
called, and had entered the narrow part of the
river again, the wind, with the sun, began to wane
and die away. It was not quite the case of a
painted ship ; we still had the current left and
a little zephyr,—the ʳcombined influence of both
brought us to the mouth of the Richelieu at Sorel.

The entrance to the river is made difficult by a
sand-bar, which runs to a considerable distance
across its mouth, the consequence of which is

that all vessels have to make a detour, and look
in so doing as if they were going to pass by the
place altogether.

On entering, we just touched, but got off
without difficulty as we had but little head-way
on. As it was after sun-down, when little birds
go to bed, the stillness was presently broken by a
shout from an inquisitive boatman, " yacht, ahoy,
what is your name ? " As soon as he heard my voice
said, " ha, I know you," and then came out to us,
and pointed out our berth for the night, where
we would be safe from any disturbance in the
form of big ships running us down. The anchor
was let go, sails lowered and furled, and preparations were made for tea.

The log was not forgotten, as it was opened and
every incident was religiously noted down.

Sorel is beautifully situated at the confluence of
two rivers, not by any means of equal size, as the
Richelieu river is not more than a few hundred
yards wide, and is an outlet to Lake Champlain
(of which more in the sequel). Sorel numbers
7,500 inhabitants, all of whom, w'th the excep-
tion of one or two families, are French. This fact
must explain why such a beautiful situation and
the great natural advantages of the place, both for
a commercial centre and shipping port (being so
far by forty-five miles nearer the sea), is what it is
at the present day—a dead-and-a-live French vil-

lage. There is a very fine square in the centre of the place, and several magnificent pine groves in the environs.

There are few towns or villages that have not some event to which the inhabitants thereof can look forward—for instance the arrival or departure of a train or steamboat. Here everybody, worth calling anybody, may be seen on the wharf at about ten o'clock p.m., to see the Montreal and Quebec boats arrive and depart. This event appears to be one of no little importance, if one may judge from the number of people present, *une grande foule.* At 10.15 p.m., three deep-toned growling whistles, announced that the boat was about to turn the corner: a bright head-light was then seen, and presently she moved up to the wharf in style. It has often been remarked with what accurate judgment the pilot brings her in. In half a minute's time the gangway is shot out upon the wharf, and immediately trucks innumerable are plying between the boats and the freight-shed, propelled by men who appear to be actuated by the spirit of magic.

Bed-time, the cabin lamp is lighted. The log reads as follows :

Thursday, August 5.—Weighed anchor at Longueuil at 2.15 p.m. Sailed away under full main-sail and jib. Wind N. N. W., light and fitfull. Ther. 78°, Baro. 31. Came to moorings at Sorel at 6.30 p. m. Distance sailed, forty-five miles.

Friday, August 6.—Ther. 74°, Baro. steady.
Six o'clock a. m., time for a swim. Small boy sculls
me to a respectful distance from civilization.
The boy, strange to say, also goes in but does
not take a header, as he cannot swim a stroke.
After these ablutions, which tend to sharpen
the appetite, we had breakfast. Oh how well
the marmalade tasted on good brown bread. The
look-out pronounced a light south wind, so we
took no time in getting under way. The wind
freshened. If it had only been blowing in any
other direction, an Irishman might have remarked, it would have been different! but as it
was it was dead against us, and the river narrow the short tacks were laborious, to say the
least. Having accomplished three miles we hove
to and went ashore for the purpose of running across milk, which we finally succeeded
in doing.

We accomplished about ten miles up the river
that afternoon, and then anchored with reluctance,
not having reached our destination at St. Ours.
By 10 o'clock, all lights except the anchor light at
the mast-head were out, and the crew, without
having established a port or starboard watch, were
sleeping the sleep of the just.

Saturday, August 7.—Fine morning. Saw the
towers of the church in St. Ours about a mile
distant, a beautiful sight, as they were being

tipped with the golden rays of the rising sun. After the usual matutinal bath and breakfast we got a tow-line out, and started, the wind having quite forgotten to blow.

St. Ours, what can be said of it ? It is a French village, the reader will understand what that means: a huge church will be pictured by the imagination, with nice, neat white cottages, and one country road running through it. We had not very long to wait before what we were waiting for appeared, namely, a tow. It looked like a long sea-serpent slowly bending its lazy length around the turns of the river. The skipper bided his time, then gave the order to cast loose from the wharf, and, after judging distance, ordered the crew, when near enough to the last barge, to ship the sweeps. A line was then thrown by the man on the barge, who made it fast in the proper manner. Connecting ourselves thus to this slowly moving body we were relieved as to any further anxiety about our progress. Of course a pipe was indulged in, together with a luxuriant lounge. Sailing naturally would have been preferable, but there was not enough wind to blow a candle out. After we had proceeded in this manner about two and a half miles, we reached the locks. This place is really pretty. Magnificent, large, spreading trees may be seen, both on the main-land and island, and the solid masonry composing the locks afforded a

pleasing variety for the eye to rest upon. We
continued on up the river after all the barges had,
in turn, got through. St. Denis and St. Antoine,
the former on the left bank, and the latter on the
right, both pretty French villages, were passed.
Then further up, St. Charles was reached, not far
from Bœil. As darkness had set in when we
reached the place, we did not see the last-
mentioned village.

There were two young men of swarthy hue on
board the barge who afforded us much amusement
by diving off into the river from a height of at least
fourteen feet while the tow was in motion. You
must not imagine that the barges are that height:
it was the lumber piled upon them that made the
difference. Their mode of procedure was to
swim ashore, and run along the bank in order to
get sufficiently far up stream to enable them to
swim back again to the barge they had left.
They had to do this because the total speed
through the water attained by these tows is about
five miles an hour, therefore the time taken to dive,
and return to the surface again had to be made up,
in the manner described, by running along the
banks.

When we had proceeded a little farther up stream
we noticed a man accompanied by his son and
daughter in a light skiff quietly taking an evening row. Presently he was seen overhauling us

with the addition of his wife and another child ; he pulled alongside for a social chat. On the principle that all things on this sublunary sphere must end, he made a motion to get his oars, that was the time to offer him a drink : considering the responsible charge which rested upon his shoulders, we gave him lemonade with a very small stick in it of a few drops of whiskey.

Another diversion presented itself to us in the form of a merry-go-round. At first we could not make out what it was, as it looked with its lamps in the darkness like miniature comets playing tag on earth. It is a good thing that the people in these parts have not forgotten how to make themselves merry. A pretty good brass band was clashing away in all sorts of time. It must have been about this stage of the proceedings that we all fell asleep. As the small boy was nearly always asleep, no doubt he was a lineal descendant of the Fat Boy mentioned in " Pickwick." When we awoke in the morning the barges all appeared as if on a spree, the tow seemed utterly demoralized. A stern wind had sprung up during the night, while the steam tug was waiting for daylight to take them through the drawbridge The *modus operandi* is to get the barges, which were previously coupled together, in line, in order to get through the narrow draw. As far as we were concerned, the wind had nearly succeeded in driving our stern on shore.

It is a very curious sight to witness. The tow is made, of course, twice as long, by being uncoupled, and, as the reader may imagine, the slow rate of speed, together with the stern wind, caused the barges to be at obtuse angles to each other. How can they get through? is the natural question. They do pass the draw, however, and that is about all that we can say with reference to it. When on the other side, the barges are put into couples again. Of course all this takes up a great deal of time, but then with an easy conscience and good digestion one can afford to forget the hurry and bustle, the feverish excitement of those, the object of whose lives is represented by dollars. As these thoughts were suggesting themselves to our minds we saw an express train dashing along enveloped in smoke and dust. How many bright, animated countenances could one find in those cars? not many. The close air, together with the noise and rattle of the train, must undoubtedly have caused sleepless nights to not a few. Our age is an age of accelerated motion—a fast and a short life.

At noon we reached Chambly basin, and anchored not far from the shore, out of the way of boats and tugs. I went ashore to send a telegram, and my friend to enquire for letters and to obtain butter, as we had run short.

In the afternoon we received visits from friends and accepted invitations to spend the evening on land. We took tea in the hotel, and from the windows had a fine view of the bay, lying like Nature's mirror, reflecting the snowy clouds floating above. The yacht, too, looked a picture as she rode at anchor without a movement, with the sails furled, and everything in its place, tidy and trim. We also saw the boy appearing from the cabin every now and then, looking as if he was trying to realize where he was

Monday, Aug. 9.—Another fine day. I hastened ashore to engage a horse to tow us through the canal, and also to get my clearance papers made out, after which we took our turn, and entered the locks. Great care must be taken to prevent the yacht from bumping against the sides, as the water is let in all at once, apparently without the slightest reference to the size or build of the craft which is passing through. The duty of rebuking fell to me, being owner ; and on one occasion the rebuke took the form of very strong language very much emphasized. We had been towed up to a lock, and while waiting for a barge to be let out a contretemps occurred. The owner of the animal had hold of the tow line, and on perceiving that his horse was walking off in the opposite direction, gave the rope to our boy; the water came with such force when the gate was opened, that it began to swing us round. I jumped ashore, seized the tow-line, and was pulling with all my might

when it gave way, dropping me with violence
on my back ; the force of the water caused our
craft to be thrown violently in the other direction,
thereby jamming the dingy and splitting the rudder.
The damage would have been more serious had
not my friend stood to his duty like a man and
eased the squeeze to the skiff with the boat hook,
which snapped in his hands. It was truly a
morning of accidents, for no sooner had this little
excitement blown over than we were plunged
into another. A mad dog happening to pass by
that way, in its eccentricity peculiar to the canine
breed in that state, made for the man's boy, and
bit him very severely in two places.

The dog disappeared as suddenly as he came,
which accounted for the fact of his present
existence, as otherwise he would have been shot.
The injured lad was taken on board and supplied
with a sponge and water, while our boy, delighting
in variety, mounted the horse, and on we went.
We had a very close shave further on. A large
empty barge was being towed down, and, as we
approached, we noticed that it was not sufficiently
in the middle or to the other side, to give us room
to pass between it and the bank ; the fact is the
wind was blowing across the canal, and blowing
it on to us ; we could not avoid it, it was too late
to take the other side. So as we came on, their
tow-line was slackened for us to pass over, and

then we saw the opening between the barge and the bank growing gradually less every moment; a shout, however, caused the boy to put the horse to a gallop, and we just shot through with a slight scrape on our port side. It was like a rat going through a hole.

At St. Johns we went ashore, having previously found a safe berth for the yacht and bought a store of provisions, also provided ourselves with a minute and comprehensive chart of Lake Champlain, which was lent to us by a kind friend. On our return to St. Johns, homeward-bound, among the manifold things we had left undone, was the neglect to report ourselves to the custom house authorities.

Having previously notified the man whose business it is to attend to the drawbridge, that we were going through, and had not a horn to blow as a warning, when we came into view, with all sail set; we saw the huge bridge swinging on its hinges, and having reached it there was room enough for us to pass straight through. Once on the other side, we felt as a fox might feel when, having doubled upon the voracious pack and excited huntsmen, he finds himself in peace and safety. We had left behind us the bumpings and scrapings in the locks, mad dogs, and the evil machinations of man, to find before us a clear reach of unencumbered water, lined on one side with trees and

dotted on the other with groves.   A fresh wind
was blowing, which carried us on at a good rate
of speed, affording to the sailors that delicious
sensation caused by the pitching of the yacht;
then again the feeling that we were progressing
on our cruise was gratifying.   Presently a sail
ahead was discerned which, through the glass,
looked like a cat-rigged yacht (*i.e.*, a sailing-
boat with only one sail attached to the mast
which is placed near the stem or bow) ; she had a
reef in her main-sail.   This beautiful reach of water
continues for six miles, when two lighthouses
were observed on the right—a short one in front,
with a tall one a little distance behind it.   This
arrangement is to enable the pilot at night to get
the two lights in line to steer by.   At this point
the river opens out to over twice the width of the
part we had sailed through.

Then, after sailing eight miles, we came to Isle-
aux-Noix.

CHAPTER II.

ISLE-AUX-NOIX.

Isle-aux-Noix is an island full of historical interest in the war of Independence.   Commanding
the approach into Canada by its situation in the

middle of the Richelieu, it proved a very formidable obstacle in the way to the incursions of the enemy. It is situated between six and seven miles from the border line. The fort is composed of earth works thrown up, with a wide moat running all around. Within are to be seen barracks of fine cut masonry, placed on three sides of a square, with a level parade-ground in the centre. There are two drawbridges over the moat, and altogether the place at present is in a very tolerable state of repair. In the year 1759, Bourlamarque, a brave officer under the command of Montcalm, seeing that it would be utter madness to attempt to make defence against overwhelming numbers, destroyed his fortifications at Crown Point on Lake Champlain, and retreated down the lake to assemble his forces, and make a stand at the Isle-aux-Noix for the protection of Montreal and the Province.

Silence now guards the place, no sound of bugle-call awakes the stillness, all is quiet save when the birds their carols sing.

An old pensioner is keeper of the place, and lives in a part of the barracks formerly called the Officers' Quarters. The island now is entirely given over to the purposes of agriculture. There have been no detachments of military there since the year 1870.

We continued on our course, somewhat doubtful

as to the channel, for the light-houses behind us
were invisible in the distance. In addition there
was a mat of weeds near the island which naturally
caused anxiety to the crew. However, we sailed
out of them without running aground. Weeds
are not necessarily an indication of shallow water,
as they grow to such a length : the regular boat
channel brings one through them. The river from
the island upward is no longer straight as it was,
but winding, therefore we kept a good look-out
for the channel. We had proceeded about two and
a half miles when we discovered by her pennant,
the Commodore's yacht in the distance. Three
cheers ! ! We felt as if we had run across a friend,
a friendly sail to a weary mariner, or any other
such simile. Now we had a definite object in
view, something in particular to sail for. On
sailing in, as it were, to our chief's waters, we
saluted by hauling our colors down and up three
times.

Camp Lodge, for such is the name of the place
which constituted our friend's summer retreat,
occupies one of the prettiest points on the whole
river. It is on high ground, well covered with
acacia trees, and has a commanding view of the
river both ways; a dining table is placed among
the trees, with awnings hung from branch to branch
on high to insure a constant shade. A ferry-
boat plies between the place and the opposite

shore; this is because a road ends here. There
is a sketch in the form of a description of one of
these ferry-boats further on.

Dismal howlings and discordant shrieks are often
heard by day and night; they are not caused by
either the demented or dying, but by the im-
patient and travel-stained wanderer, who, upon
seeing an abrupt termination placed before him in
the form of water, shouts for deliverance from
stagnation. There is no definite period allotted to
that sort of thing (the howling entreaties, I mean,)
for it depends upon the ferryman, whether or
not he cares to bestir himself. Such is the state
of things where monopoly reigns without op-
position.

We were most hospitably received on shore at
the Lodge. Rival experiences were recounted on
each side, with strict adherence to the truth, for
I may safely assert we had none of that class
called fish-story-tellers among us—simply the
truth, and nothing but the truth.

After having spent a pleasant evening we
hailed the yacht, and presently shooting towards
us over the dark waters, we saw the dingy propelled by our cabin-boy, who no doubt felt
aggrieved at being thus awakened.

Tuesday, Aug. 10.—Fine clear weather. At
eleven o'clock we bade adieu to our friends and
sailed away for the lake, eight miles distant. We

had passed Hospital Island when a very strong
cats-paw struck us, so much stronger than the
preceding gusts that the starbord stay-buckle snapped, causing the mast to list over four or five inches
out of the perpendicular, and if we had capsized,
my friend, who was at the time in the cabin, would
have been in a bad place ; some of the ballast shifted, and altogether it was a close thing. The reader
may be excused for making the following mental
observations : " Serves him right, for having the
main sheet fastened." " Of course that is the
way that all yachting accidents happen," etc.

My dear friend, the sheet was not made fast,
as I had it in my hands at the time, and allowed it
to run-out as the wind struck the sail. To my
non-nautical friends I will remark that a sheet
is the rope which is attached to the main boom in
a cutter or sloop, and controls the main-sail when
hoisted. Not having upset, we breathed, instead
of sputtering in the water, as we otherwise should
have done. The next thing was to have a new
stay-buckle made; having run into the wind, immediately on being struck by the gust, we let go
the anchor. We had no time to lose as I had an
appointment at Philipsburg, Missisiquoi Bay, the
next day, so I took the dingy, and rowed ashore.
Having made a bargain with a man to have a new
one procured from Lacolle, I then returned on
board. We had not long to wait, the man appeared

with a new stay-buckle, which was immediately adjusted, and on we went.

When we reached Bloody Island we saw Fort Montgomery, four or five miles off, and the railway-bridge at Rouse's Point.

I must say that the names of the islands we passed were not altogether what might be called sweet-sounding names, but, on the contrary, rather suggestive of suffering and murder. Why these names should have been given to them, remains a mystery ; perhaps it may be accounted for in this way : their discovery was during the bloody Indian wars between Champlain and the Iroquois, and their appellations, if not applied then, might have been in more recent wars during the time of Montcalm, or in the year 1775, when the war for American Independence began.

Here the river broadens again to somewhat the same width as before we reached Isle-aux-Noix.

Fort Montgomery is just on the line, on the American side, and commands a position which affords for its guns a good sweep down the river. As it stands now, with blessed Peace folding it in its beneficent arms, nothing formidable, or even striking, presents itself to view. Strangers, however, are not allowed to visit it,—it cannot be from caution lest the outside world should get acquainted with the secrets entombed within its walls, yet, what motive can they have ? If visitors were admitted, tipping would go some way in paying a man to

look after the place. Of course that would be a
very small consideration; but then the question
remains, why are people not allowed to visit it ?
Such gigantic strides have been made in the art
of war, and in the science of manufacturing in-
fernal machines for the destruction of precious
human life since Fort Montgomery was built,
that it would be difficult to conceive of anything
new being found within.

However, we passed it unchallenged, carrying at our mast-head the Dominion Ensign. It
naturally makes a person feel important when
he sees any great preparation going on, or
a good deal of trouble being taken for himself. So
we felt when, after holding a straight course for
the drawbridge, we saw it slowly opening to let
us through, and through we went, on the same
tack, thanking the man at the grind out of cour-
tesy. We sailed past the old wharf into the
harbor in front of the custom house, and moored
alongside a very extensive and apparently ne-
glected wharf. We experienced little difficulty
in finding the authorities we were in search of.
After introducing ourselves and explaining our
purpose, an official, a very pleasant man, came
down with us to the yacht, more as a matter of
form than from curiosity to see that we had not any
dutiable articles on board. A parting drink, and a
good shake of the hand was the result, and off
we sailed, light-hearted as a boy from school.

There were now before us eight miles of an open expanse of water to sail over. We had a good stern wind, and consequently sailed with main sail and spinnaker; the sails thus arranged give the appearance of a sloop sailing along like a crab, sideways. On leaving Rouse's Point, where we had interviewed the custom house official, it was ascertained that we had about thirty miles to traverse before reaching Philipsburg, which was our next port.

It may be remarked that on entering an extensive sheet of water a yacht appears to participate in the feelings of those on board. Having been confined to the narrow limits and swift currents of rivers, on passing into a lake she jumps for joy upon the sparkling, white-crested waves, and seems to pull herself together for a sail in earnest. When distances of ten, fifteen, and twenty miles intervene between shore and shore, and there is an appearance of a good blow, with perhaps a falling barometer, it makes it still more important for her to go her best.

Then the yachtsman and crew feel as if they were looking upon a thing animated with life, the spray dashing from her bows as she danced along. Then, when she keels over to a gust, looking as if wrestling for dear life with some unknown fury, we feel

"The exulting sense, the pulse's maddening sway
That thrills the traveller on his trackless way."

CHAPTER III.

WEDNESDAY, *August* 11.—6 a. m. No wind.—
Weather hot and sultry, a very annoying state of
things, as I had to be in Philipsburg that day,
and there lay before us sixteen miles. We had
accomplished over fifteen miles yesterday in little
over five hours, sailing half the time with next to
no wind. At Alburgh Point the wind left us, and
then we only went three miles in about as many
hours, to a pretty spot by a ferry, where we
anchored for the night.

From Alburgh Point, the entrance to Missisquoi Bay is through a narrow arm of the lake,
which appears like a river except for its total
absence of current. We passed several ferries
which were entirely new to us. What is under-
stood by a ferry-boat on this lake is a flat-bottom
scow with a mast on one side, also keel boards
fastened to the sides towards each end. This is,
of course, to take the place of a regular keel and
prevent the boat from making what in nautical
language is called lee-way. The boatman steers
from either end by means of a sweep. Toll is

nominally fifteen cents for each person, twenty-five cents for a single carriage or buggy, and forty cents for a double team.

Well, as I said before, there was hardly any wind. The prospect looked very blue, as far as the keeping of the promise to be at the trysting place was concerned. Two good-sized pike fell to our lot, having been hooked during ten minutes trolling. We then made sail and started. The wind was not only light, but against us, the consequence was large tacks had to be made. It was a sweltering day ; oh, how hot it was ! with no wind to blow away the roasting atmosphere which appeared to be getting up to fever heat.

A very curious circumstance occurred after we had passed the railway-bridge and Alburgh Springs, which is worthy of note. We had taken to the sweeps, and were toiling away like galley slaves, allotting, as is generally the case under such circumstances, the time that each man should occupy in his turn at the grind ; when, on looking to the nor'ard, we perceived a distinct line of dark waters, extending for miles across the lake, coming down on us ; we looked upon this as a regular God-send, for it enabled us to keep our engagement with our friends and relatives who had driven fourteen miles to meet us. Therefore, instead of coming in at the finish, like dogs with their tongues hanging out of their mouths with fatigue, we came in upon the crested waves, which we were told by the way was *such a pretty sight.*

Thursday, Aug. 12.—Anchored off Philipsburg —weather showing signs of a change; Thermometer still high ; Barometer falling.

The rudder had to be slightly repaired, to prevent its catching weeds, which materially retarded our way through the water; after that, together with the time taken to clean the yacht, we sailed away at twelve o'clock for Alburgh Springs, with a nice fair breeze.

There was nothing very remarkable about the place beyond the fact that there were two large hotels there, and holiday people in the act of working off the effects of bad-tasting water by indulging in that novel pastime of playing croquet. We anchored at the old ferry again that night, and had quite a sociable chat with the ferryman.

Friday, August 13.—At an early hour, we resumed our voyage and soon reached Pelots Bay. This Bay is remarkable for its good camping ground and anchorage for yachts and steam launches.

From six to a dozen nice, wooden, square-built houses, or huts as they are called, line the shore upon which ripples the crystal water. We noticed a steam yacht called " Ella," and were invited to go over her. She was a picture as she rode at an-

chor with her side awnings down. The yacht is
acknowledged to be a model in every sense of the
word, and here our description ends, as space and
time will not permit of any account which could
do her justice.

At one o'clock we weighed anchor and sailed
for Plattsburg, distance fifteen miles. The wind
was dead ahead and gusty. We sailed quite close
to Isle La Motte, which is celebrated in all the
historical records of the Lake. At four o'clock,
after a total calm, during which time we were
tossed up and down with sails flapping, the
wind veered round from south-west to north-west,
and we noticed that the barometer had fallen.
After hot, sultry weather these indications of a
storm of some kind made us look for a convenient
place to cast anchor in, which we did by running
in about a mile. After watching the weather, and
comparing what we saw with former storms, we
weighed anchor, and ran across from Long Point to
Gravelly Point, a distance of about four and a half
miles, in thirty-three minutes. We escaped a duck-
ing from the fact that nothing gave away about
the rigging and also that the movable ballast kept
its place. With a sense of relief we rounded to,
let go anchor, and furled the sails for the night.
If the historical records are correct a drink of something mixed with water was indulged in as com-
memoration of the successful undertaking.

Our cabin-boy Johnny announced the fact that there was no more milk aboard. The dingy was brought alongside, and off went the skipper and friend with a trolling line astern. A black bass was hooked, yes, sir, actually hooked ! ! ! by no particular desire of its own. If the fish would, by some unaccountable accident, occupy the position which brought him right across our line, how could he avoid it. However, poor little fish fell a victim to circumstances over which he had no control and not to gluttony, which, alas ! is too often the sad fate of the finny tribe. The cock-pit (that is the after-part between the cabin and rudder post) was converted into a species of tent, by throwing rubber sheets over the boom of the main-sail. At five o'clock in the morning we were greeted by a deluge of rain—a sort of rain which would have done credit to the time of Noah. Drops at first, followed by small streams of water made their way between the sheets. The cabin did not leak fortunately. It was greatly regretted by the captain that a regular awning had not been procured before starting, which would have kept the water out. However, one was ordered next day as soon as Plattsburg was reached.

CHAPTER IV.

SATURDAY, *August* 13.—Storm blowing off. Wind
from the west; a good high sea running in the
middle of the lake. Thermometer 76; barometer
rising. Could not tell exactly what time it was
when I awoke; seemed to have been awake
all night, barring a few winks taken, " promiscuous-
like," between the drops of rain.

We got under way about nine a.m., and sailed
round the point along the lee-shore, where the
wind was very fitful; but when we rounded
Cumberland Point we got the full effect of both the
wind and high sea. The feeling was, *in for it, sink
or swim.* The wind was pretty strong, but not very
squally; there were certainly gusts, but we were
on the look-out. It turned out a fine run, the yacht
did her work well, and in good form. We ran
in on two tacks, and anchored not far from the
breakwater opposite Plattsburg at 10.15 a.m.
Distance sailed, nine miles.

Our yachting toggery in this place excited a
good deal of rude staring on the part of the inhabitants. One man said to another, " Well, that
is the first Royal Marine I ever saw." A place
for everything and everything in its place is
an old motto. A dress for everything is equally
applicable. Who would expect to see a yachtsman in a top-hat and a black coat ?

Plattsburg is situated at the end of a bay. Fouquet's hotel near the station and wharf, has very pretty grounds on one side of it. It was not long before two of the crew might have been seen following a small boy, carrying on his head a huge basket which contained provisions for the yacht.

An account of Plattsburg, written in 1860, is as follows:—A township, and village, and capital of Clinton county, N. Y., on Cumberland Bay, an indentation of Lake Champlain. It is situated at the mouth of the Saranac river, on both sides of which the village is built. Population 6,680. The river affords valuable water privileges, and there are several manufactories. Extensive barracks, about one mile from the village, formerly occupied by government troops, are now used for the annual agricultural fairs. On September 11, 1814, the Americans gained a memorable naval victory over the English near this place.

Sunday, August 14.—Fine bright morning, promise of clear weather. Thermometer 77; barometer steadily going up. Church parade in *mufti.* In the afternoon, cabin-boy, not having forgotten early religious instruction, went to Sunday-school. My friend also went ashore, so I kept afternoon watch on board, and occupied my time in the following manner. I will now give you a description of Lake Champlain and the naval engagement between the British and American forces, in order to occupy my time, and afford you, kind reader, information which, if you have not previously acquired it, may prove interesting.

Lake Champlain is a picturesque sheet of water lying between the State of New York, and extending from Whitehall, in the former State, to St. Johns in Canada. It is 120 miles long, and varies in breadth from forty rods to fifteen miles. Its greatest breadth unobstructed by islands is about ten miles, at a point near Burlington, Vermont. Its depth varies from fifty-four to two hundred and eighty-two feet, and vessels of eighty or one hundred tons burden navigate its whole extent. The principal islands which adorn its surface are North Hero, eleven miles by two in area; South Hero, thirteen by four, and La Motte, six by two; these three with several smaller ones, and the peninsula of Alburgh, all in the northern part, form the county of Grande Isle, in Vermont. The largest rivers entering the lake are the Missisquoi, Onion or Winooski, Lamoille, Otter, Chazy, Saranac (the old Indian for the lake itself), Au Sable, and the outlet of Lake George in the southwest part. Its own outlet is the Sorel, or Richelieu river, which empties into the St. Lawrence at Sorel, and with the Chambly canal affords a passage for vessels of large size to the ocean. In reference to the south end, there is water communication for barges with the Hudson river. Navigation is usually closed by ice about the end of November, and opens early in spring, generally the second week in April.

The waters abound with bass, pickerel, salmon trout, perch, and other varieties of fish. This lake, filling a valley enclosed by high mountains, is celebrated for its magnificent scenery, embracing the Green Mountains of Vermont on the eastern side, and the Adirondac Mountains of New York State on the western. Several pleasant villages and watering places, with one or two important towns, are situated on its shores, and at the present day well-kept farms and picturesque farm buildings adorn its sloping banks.

Even as far back as 1857, the aggregate tonnage enrolled and licensed was 10,550 ; value of imports, $5,043,595; value of exports, $2,965,532; number of vessels entered was 1,878 ; total tonnage, 122, 543. At the present day it can easily be imagined how these figures would be multiplied by the enormous increase of traffic since the year 1857. In 1880, although there is such an amount of freight carried to and from the States by three different lines of railway, yet the carrying of coal to Canada and the exporting of lumber to the States is in proportion as briskly pushed forward as the railway carrying freight is.

Lake Champlain was discovered in the year

1600 by Samuel Champlain, whose name it received. Samuel Champlain's experience may be cited as follows :—" Again the canoes advanced, the river widening as they went ; great islands appeared, leagues in extent : Isle la Motte, Long Island, Grande Isle. Channels where ships might float and broad reaches of expanding water stretched between the islands, and Champlain entered the lake which preserves his name to posterity. Cumberland Head was passed, and from the opening of the great channel between Grande Isle and the mainland, he could look forth upon what appeared to be a sea. Edged with woods, the tranquil flood spread southward beyond his sight. Far on the left, the forest ridges of the Green Mountains were heaved against the sky, patches of snow still glistening on their tops ; and on the right rose the Adirondacks, haunts in these later years of amateur sportsmen from counting-rooms, or college halls ; nay of adventurous beauty, with sketch-book and pencil.

At night Champlain and his party encamped again. The scene is a familiar one to many a tourist and sportsman ; and perhaps standing at sunset on the peaceful strand, Champlain saw what a roving student of this generation has seen on these same shores, at the same hour,—the glow of the vanished sun behind the western mountains, darkly piled in mist and shadow along the sky ;

near at hand, the dead pine, mighty in decay, stretching its ragged arms athwart the burning heaven, the crow perched on its top like an image carved in jet; and aloft the night-hawk, circling in his flight, and with a strange whirring sound diving through the air each moment for the insects he makes his prey."

This lake has been the scene of many important events in the early wars of the continent, especially so when in the year 1814 it became celebrated in the military history of the United States by the victory of the Americans over the British. At that time an invasion of the northern portion of New York was contemplated, and a force of from 10,000 to 15,000 troops was collected in the vicinity of Montreal for that purpose. In such an expedition the possession of Lake Champlain became an object of great importance, as it flanked the march of the invading army for more than ten miles, thus offering great facilities for the transportation of reinforcements and supplies.

The efforts of both armies were therefore directed to the creation of naval forces on the lake in the shortest time possible, and vessels were built and equipped for the service with magical rapidity.

The largest American vessel, called the " Saratoga," was built at Vergennes; the time taken to build her was forty days. In August, 1814, the English army, about 12,000 strong, commanded by Sir George Prévost, advanced in four divisions against Plattsburg, at that time held by Brigadier-General Macomb, with a force of about 2,000. Captain McDonough, who commanded the American naval force on the lake, anchored in Plattsburg Bay on September 3rd, and awaited the appearance of the enemy's squadron, which came down the lake on Sir George Prévost's left flank. Cumberland Head is the most northern point of Plattsburg Bay ; and about a quarter of a league from it, in a south-west direction, lies Crab Island, small and low, and surrounded by an extensive shoal. Upon this island a battery of one gun was established.

The total American force consisted of fourteen vessels, mounting in all eighty-six guns, and carrying about eight hundred and fifty officers and men, including a small detachment of soldiers acting as mariners. The British squadron was commanded by Captain Downie, an officer of distinction, and was composed of sixteen vessels mounting ninety-five guns, and carrying about nine hundred and fifty officers and men.

On the morning of September 11, 1814, just after the sun had risen, the approach of the British squadron was discovered by the guard-boats of the Americans, and preparations were made for action. Soon after eight o'clock, the English having formed in line, approached the American squadron in good order, the wind moderate and fair, the weather fine.

As the British approached, the Americans brought their broadsides to bear, and a few moments passed in silence and expectation.

The water was smooth, the ships were within point blank range, and the guns were sighted with accuracy. This single broadside killed and wounded about forty men on the "Saratoga." After this the engagement became animated and very sanguinary, which is easily accounted for by the fact that the vessels were very heavily armed, and their crews numerous in proportion to their size. In fact, says the writer, they more nearly resembled floating batteries than vessels of war.

The American loss, in killed and wounded, was one hundred and eleven. That of the English was variously stated at from one hundred and seventy-three to two hundred. This strange victory for the Americans brought in its train more important results for them than any other naval achievements in that century.

I was just trying to unravel this mystery of the defeat of the English when "Eurydice ahoy ! !! " was echoed over the water by the rest of the crew, the watch was over, and likewise revery gave place to stern necessity, and to tea.

Monday morning, Aug. 15.—Fine day, with a propitious wind. We were anxious to be off, but were detained until eleven o'clock waiting for the awning which had been ordered on the Saturday previous. We set to work with a hearty good will, unfurled the sails, and made preparations for a start.

Already the main sail is flapping impatiently in the wind. "Stand by the anchor chain." "Haul away." The chain cable is stowed, after which the jib is hoisted, "stand by the jib halyards," "haul away:—avast:--belay." And away she glides before a gentle north-west breeze. Plattsburg is rapidly receding in our wake, and we are nearing Valcour's Island on the starboard bow, and Crab on the port. It may here be remarked that the former Island, in the year 1874, was the camping ground of a Free Love community. Like all such mad schemes since the primitive days of Adam, it did not hold together long; at all events, six years after, a powerful field glass failed to reveal the slightest vestige of a petticoat, or anything that looked like black trousers any where on the island. Our cruise was either too late, or they broke up too soon (probably a little of both), for us to interview those curious people. Crab Island is the burial ground of sailors and mariners who fell in the battle of Plattsburg, in the year 1814. "After life's fitful fever he sleeps well," not even awakened by the rippling of the wavelets caused by the gentle breeze upon its shore, nor yet by the white crested billows storm tossed upon its rocks.　Our musings are soon terminated by the jibbing of the boom as it swings across to the other side.　All right if you will have it so : we are indifferent about what tack it shall be, provided the wind does not leave us all together.

Nothing can more fitly resemble indecision in human nature than this jibbing about of the boom : now on one side, then swinging over to the other. Besides being a silly proceeding either in man or yacht, it is decidedly unpleasant, and unproductive of any progress.

The wind, however, does during a short interval leave us.　Whether it is the close proximity to the island or not, we cannot tell.　Our course was taken for the open lake to provide for such contingency.　The wind eventually settles down in a different quarter, and the foam is once more seen whitening her bow.　Port Kent is our stopping place.　The chart is consulted.　Yes, quite right, that place is down on the chart as a reef.　The reef is avoided.　The next question is, in what direction are we to steer for Port Kent ? On comparing the formation of the shore with the markings on the chart, we find that we are about to pass the place, consequently the yacht's course is altered, and now the anchor chain is heard running out.　The jib is lowered, and then after the anchor has taken firm hold, the main-sail is run down.　Johnny, whose illustrious name has already figured in the log, is left on board to make all straight, by furling the sails and getting ready for our midday meal, a task for which he is nearly always prepared, and one which appears to give him great joy. It may here be remarked in extenuation, that yachting greatly sharpens the appetite.

Au Sable Chasm is three miles inland from Port Kent. The crew were informed that the stupendous grandeur of the place vied with all that is wonderful to be seen in Niagara, and were consequently induced to go. A deep chasm averaging 175 feet, with water flowing now over shallow places and again through deep fissures, trends its way for about a mile and a half. At short distances there are chasms crossing the large one, and also caves. There is a devil's ride, a fairy glen, and somebody else's pulpit, but apart from these familiar epithets the place is truly grand. There is Jacob's Well formed originally by a small waterfall; they are at present taking earth out of it, and have got to the depth of twenty feet. Towards the end of this marvellous chasm there is a flat bottom boat moored. The guide takes his place at the stern, and steers the party over some rapids to the end. A most peculiar effect is produced by the narrow stratum of stone which runs in parallel lines at an angle a few degrees from the level of the water. The effect of this

is to make the water appear to be on the down
ward slant. It was remarked by several that we
were going down hill. The depth of the water
in some places is sixty-five feet.

Another curious feature of the place may be
noted, namely, that there are several manufacturing establishments at the head of the chasm, two
rolling mills, a pulp factory, &c.

> " Along the cool sequestered vale of life
> They keep the noiseless tenor of their way."

Only noiseless in so far as nature is concerned,
for one could easily imagine a pretty good racket
in the vicinity of a nail factory.

There is a large hotel standing alone on high
ground; we found on enquiring that it was the
summer resort of a good many people. At first sight
one is surprised, and speculates what can induce
travellers to visit the place, but on closer investi-
gation, in addition to the wonders of the chasm,
the country is hilly, the air bracing, and the view
of the lake is grand.

We returned to Port Kent, eight miles distant,
and found, to our relief, that the yacht and boy
were there in the same place we had left them.

CHAPTER V.

" She walks the waters like a thing of life,
And seems to dare the elements to strife."

BYRON.

Tuesday, Aug. 16.—Hazy ; thermometer high ;
barometer down since yesterday morning. Got
under way early, and started for a run into the
middle of the lake. The wind was fresh, but not
altogether favorable for Burlington. On nearing
that extraordinary rock called "Rocky Dunder,"
we were very much struck by its peculiar shape.
No vegetation adorns it. If it had not been blowing quite so hard, a nearer approach could have
been effected, and a closer scrutiny would have
satisfied our curiosity. However, as we saw it in
the distance it looked like a lone sentinel guarding
through all weathers the eternal mysteries of the
hidden deep. It formerly served as a boundary
mark between the Mohawks and their enemies,
the Algonquins.

We sailed out four miles and a half, and then
tacked back; it was a quick run; the fresh air
gaving us an excellent appetite.

Here, at Port Kent, we remained anchored
with nothing in particular to do for three hours,
waiting for the express to bring us letters. The
express came, but no letters. Sailed away from

our anchorage at fifteen minutes past eleven, with a reef in the mainsail; it was not long before that was slackened out, then after a little time the top-sail was hoisted.

Although the prospect at starting was good, the subsequent· reality proved the contrary. The wind left us in the middle of the lake; but owing to the total absence of any current, we sailed through the huge looking-glass water with a steady onward movement.

Our port for the night, we had decided, should be Pelots Bay, and that was situated about twenty-eight miles from the port we had just left. We relieved each other at the tiller in order to take rest in the cabin, which, although roasting, afforded shade. On shore we thought this sort of thing intolerable, so we had consolation, as we nursed the idea.

At six, we rounded the headland into Pelots Bay and, phantom-like, glided in, and took up a station out of the way of the steam yachts. I used the term phantom-like because we could not detect the slightest zephyr either on the surface of the water or on the air. After everything had been made snug, during tea we heard a silvery voice :

"Welcome back! You will come ashore presently, will you not? and you will tell us if you had a pleasant cruise." "Oh, yes; certainly, we will row ashore and see you all." The following dialogue followed this pleasing incident. "How kind of them to welcome us back in this way!!!" "Yes, indeed!! It is worth braving a thousand storms." "By Jove, we are lucky beggars to have hit upon such nice people." Each was thinking of the pretty face, but neither spoke of the individual, only of the friends in general.

The reader must remember this was our return visit to the lovely spot, consequently we were not strangers. I need not try very hard to convince you that we spent a most enjoyable evening on our friends' door-step that night; not knowing, but fearing that their bed-time might be at an early hour.

The pale, flickering moon, that has already been responsible for so much wasted energy in the endeavors of weak mortals to pour out bad poetry from their enraptured souls, did not draw us on to the extent of being poetical; but still I cannot deny that tender thoughts held possession of our minds, and gave a bias to our dreams.

> "In joyous youth, what soul hath never known
> Thought, feeling, taste, harmonious to its own?
> Who hath not paused while beauty's pensive eye
> Asked from his heart the homage of a sigh?
> Who has not owned, with rapture-smitten frame,
> The power of grace, the magic of a name?"

Wednesday, Aug. 17.—Ther. 69; Barom. falling:—A tremendous blow had arisen toward morning. We awoke with thoughts of our infancy when we were rocked to sleep by nurse. The yacht was pitching and tossing about like mad. Immediately, more cable chain was played out, and another anchor improvised to lessen the strain on the first one. We had no desire or intention to allow the wind ignominiously to cast us a wreck on shore right in front of our friends' summer residences,—the bare idea sent a shiver from head to foot. It looked like a regular two days' gale, which it subsequently proved to be.

At this period of our cruise the whole crew were unanimous in agreeing that indeed their lines had fallen in pleasant places; that surely the gods had in this event been most propitious :—we were in a most comfortable harbor. If all sailors could only be thus weather-bound there would be more Christians in the world, and fewer malcontents. The question might naturally arise, as to how we spent our time during those two days of storm. How did we spend them? The question should rather be, how can we ever forget how we spent them, reading to the ladies of course, holding skeins, telling yarns, suggesting theatricals, and smoking occasionally with the men. We left undone all manner of things, and we did all manner of things, and finally there was nothing left undone that was done.

Let me draw your attention to the steam yachts

and launches of all sizes, from thirty tons down to
half a ton, riding at anchor, ready at a moment's
notice.   There was not a single sailing yacht
among them—what is the conclusion : is this
generation getting lazy or scientific, or both ?
Perhaps it is destiny.

However, steam is certainly one of the most
prominent characteristics of the age. The " Coming
Race" may rejoice in boats propelled by electricity,
flying through the air, and, as an eminent author
has it, *Vril* may become the all-powerful medium
for the exponent of force, and motion to result
from it.   It is the opinion of the crew that nothing
can, or ever will, supersede sailing.

The question as to how we were to leave this
charming spot was still more difficult to solve on
the third morning, when we discovered that a dead
calm prevailed—but I must not anticipate.

On the afternoon of the second day, the crew of
the Eurydice were invited to join the ladies who
were going for a short steam sail, or steamboat-
ride, in one of the fastest boats for its size in the
fleet.   The storm was just beginning to blow
itself out, but for all that there was a good sea on.
It was certainly very pleasant, cutting through the
waves with a merry party on board, and we all
thoroughly enjoyed it.   That evening we went to
an impromptu concert, which was very good—so
good in fact that one of the crew did nothing but

whistle the tune of one of the songs all the way
home, which was, to say the least of it, like giving
one's self away.

Thursday, Aug. 18.—You will notice that in the
log two days have merged into one. There was
nothing new to note down with regard to the
weather.

This morning turned out fine. The mercury
in both instruments was steadily rising; the wind
was dead, having strangled itself in its fury.

It was with feelings of fond regret that we
made preparation for departure. We said adieu,
with the promise to run that way next summer :
a prospect, now so long, in retrospect so short,
ere these twelve big moons shall have gone through
the tragedy of dying, and being born again.

The yacht moved out, as she had entered three
short days ago, with all sail set, and but little
wind. We moved, and that was all :—we were
pensive, who can wonder !! At last when, like
Telemaque, we had left the enchanted spot, new
vigor seemed to fill our drooping frames, after
we had indulged in several plunges into the
deep cool lake which was, by the by, a very good
way to occupy the time, for there was no sailing
without wind, and we were not in that frame of
mind when reading does any good. There are
times when reading is out of the question, and
this was one of them. When the mind has received

deep impressions and the heart is oppressed with woe, no book, except of a most exciting charracter, is any good.

We could not go on for ever popping in and then scrambling on board again like so many monkeys at a show; the proceeding was not only fatiguing but was getting monotonous and undignified, consequently we remembered the good old adage, by the sweat of thy brow, etc., and put its maxims into practice. We took turns, as we had done on a previous occasion, at the sweeps. It is a curious thing whenever a man times his work in turn with another man the clock invariably appears to stand still in mute astonishment at the prodigious feats that are being accomplished. When my turn came, I began to have serious doubts as to whether I should keep such an erratic time-piece.

Rouse's Point, a haven of rest, is reached at last. We ran alongside the old wharf, but, after everything had been made tidy, I had the yacht removed to a little distance off as there were too many small boys looking on; they would, in all probability, have jumped on board when our backs were turned and made free in a manner peculiar to all boys.

My friend introduced me to a friend he happened to know in the place, and thus it was that we spent a pleasant evening, consuming tobacco, and telling yarns.

D

CHAPTER VI.

SATURDAY, *August* 20.—At anchor off Rouse's
Point. Fine morning; good westerly breeze;
sailed through the draw to the opposite side, and
anchored in front of the large printing establishment belonging to John Lovell & Son. This building can be seen for miles, and is the most prominent
object in the place. It is to the promoters of such
institutions as these, that man's progress through
the world's dark history has been gradually
enlightened. I cannot possibly, in the short space
which I have allotted for this log, begin to
adequately describe all, or even part, of the wonderful improvements in machinery and the different
processes employed in this building for the diffu-
sion of learning and the promotion of literature.

My friend was very kindly invited to go over
this establishment, and wisely availed himself
of the occasion, and, as he said, "not only did I see
letters being hurled together so as to form words
with magical rapidity, and the words in their turn
to form reading matter, but also other kinds of
work more wonderful still." I have been told, it
would amply repay one to travel all the way from
Montreal to see this large Printing House. When
this had been recounted to the skipper, he felt
a strong inclination to prolong the stay, and run

ashore; in addition, an invitation had been extended to us to lunch with friends; then just when the decision had been given in favor of remaining, dark clouds threatening rain warned us to weigh anchor. We accordingly sailed away before the storm, and left our friends, with regrets at not being able to see more of them The storm came on so slowly that we were enabled to reach the Commodore's camp, just as it came down in sheets. The skipper kept on all sail, for it was a race with the elements; he also kept one eye over his shoulder to detect the first indications of a blow in order to shorten sail in time. The moment the storm was on us, around we went into the wind, and down came the sails: the boy was left on board to form his conclusions as to the probable duration of the storm, and we went ashore. A warm reception, which had the effect of taking off the chill of the rain, greeted us as we rushed into the house with a bound. A substantial lunch was done thorough justice to, after which we looked for and procured good anchorage for the yacht: the storm by this time had passed over, and left the leaves with glistening tears in the sunshine.

We remained at this place until Wednesday morning: we could not get away, were not allowed in fact to think of such a thing. We messed on shore with our friends, and altogether had a capital time. Of course on Sunday we indulged in the customary afternoon lounge, there being no church, no litany service, no Sunday-school, and no ignorant ragged children to teach the pathway of safety to; we read good books, however, which was the next best thing. Johnny, our cabin boy, went fishing, horrible to relate, and met with poor success: we did not lose this excellent opportunity of pointing a moral, "The little boy who goes fishing on Sunday, and breaks his mother's heart, etc.; " we never afterwards could ascertain whether the boy was any the better either for the fishing, or for the moral to it.

The next day the skipper, wishing to afford health-ful recreation to a party of children and a few grown-up people, took a large party out for a sail. Then the following day we accompanied the Commodore on a picnic cruise to the Lake. We had a pleasant and somewhat eventful trip.

The Commodore steamed off at 9.15, and re-turned at about the same hour at night, having in the meantime traversed nearly fifty miles, making three stops, of an hour and a half to two hours, at each place. This could only be accomplished with a fast boat. Pelots Bay was visited by the crew of the Eurydice for the third time; but none of the party besides, which numbered about twenty, had ever been there before. They one and all fell victims to the mesmeric influence of the place, and like us vowed they would go there again.

" He sweeps before the wind,
  Treads the loved shore he sighed to leave behind ;
  Meets at each step a friend's familiar face,
  And flies at last to Helen's long embrace."

I must not forget 'to mention that a gun was fired as a salute, both as we entered and left the harbor ; and the dear old Union Jack was hoisted on board the largest yacht in honor of our visit. As we steamed out, the steam-whistle was sounded ; but as the wire maliciously got caught, this whistle was prolonged for a considerable period of time, awaking, no doubt, in the minds of our entertainers the thought that it was our playful way of showing our appreciation of their kin d ness and hospitality.

During our voyage, as we steamed away home - ward-bound, we stopped for a picnic tea on Isle La Motte, in spite of the indications of a coming storm, shown by the gathering clouds. The storm did not come down on us, however, until we had passed the railway-bridge at Rouse's Point, and had got into the river. The dingy was very nearly swamped, and there was a general holding on to shawls and wraps to prevent their being blown over-board. We steamed the whole way down the narrow winding river, through the inky dark- ness under full pressure, at about fourteen miles an hour, and kept up that exciting rate of speed until we ran in under the lee of Camp Lodge Point. Altogether it was a most memorable cruise, and the impressions left upon our minds will not soon be forgotten.

CHAPTER VII.

WEDNESDAY, *August* 24.—We could not have had a finer day for our departure. At six o'clock I went ashore, and shot a few snipe for an invalid ; after which, bath and breakfast.

It was happily a case of a short adieu to the Commodore's party, as they were to meet us next day at St. Johns, and tow us through the canal.

Sailed away at 11 a.m. against a head wind, which made short tacks unavoidably necessary, and consequently laborious, as ballast had to be shifted each tack, and a constant look-out kept to avoid running in too close to shore. By way of a side-note, I will remark that, during our whole cruise, we not once ran ashore, and sailed altogether four hundred and ten miles.

We came up to Isle aux Noix at about 12.15, and went ashore to have a look at the place. I left my friend talking with the caretaker of the fort, and returned to the bank of the river, where for a short space of time I luxuriated in the mid-day sun like a lizard.

vVnat a blessing it is to be free from the res-
traints of society, and the trammels of business with
its multifarious intrigues and speculations! To be
able to feel with regard to the former that you are
in no danger of running against anybody's pre-
judices, or of inadvertently making anybody un-
happy, and that Smith or Jones is not waiting for
an apology; to feel that, for the time being, you
are perfectly justified in taking this lizard-like
repose, and in thus moralizing upon the fashion of
the world. With the cool, invigorating breeze
fanning your cheek, and the ripple of waters playing against the shore at your feet; with the pleasant sound of the insects buzzing about, mingled
with chirping of birds—what could be found want-
ing to make up that Elysium of happiness except,
eprhaps, the clear musical tones of the voice we
know so well, and love so dearly :—A voice that
may be as a mere echo in the future, only awaken-
ing sweet memories of the past. Oh! world why
art thou thus so dark a riddle: to let us feel that
we ought to know, but cannot learn, the dark
intricacies of our future wanderings, or probable
fate!

" Hallo there ! What, asleep ! Too bad ; I did
not intend to keep you waiting so long,"—
thus spoke my friend: my answer was :—" I
have enjoyed basking in the sun. Have been
communing with nature,—and—and thinking

about other things—moralizing in fact. Let us get aboard, and then we will moralize upon the necessity of food to sustain animal existence." "All right," my friend replied,—the correct thing to do.

We are once more tacking backwards and forwards, from one side of the river to the other, from a distance probably looking as if we were going in for child's play, and making no headway, but in reality covering considerable ground each tack. This sort of thing went on until we had reached the narrow part of the river at the two light-houses, when the wind, in company with the bright orb of day, left us.

After tea one of the crew went ashore with a light tow-line, and towed the yacht for about an hour which, with regard to distance, might mean two and a half miles. It was a pleasant novelty, and afforded excellent exercise, trudging along the side of the river, through tall reeds, across musk-rat-holes, and into soft, miry clay. Variety is good, as long as it lasts, if it does not last too long. So we thought when towing gave place to rowing. It was not long before we dropped anchor nearly opposite the old Officers' Quarters, at St. Johns, and went ashore.

To find one's way at night over uneven ground, past yards and buildings, suggestive of barking dogs, bent on mischief, is both difficult, and unpleasant. Either the one or other contingent is ever before you—to fall headlong into a ditch, or be bitten and consequently die of hydrophobia : fortunately, we neither met with, or even heard, the bark of the dog, nor were we blind leaders of the blind, as neither of us fell into a ditch. Presently alighting on the level road, we walked into the principal street of St. Johns. No letters to be had, even if there were any for us, as the Post Office was closed for the night, consequently we went to the hotel to get news.

The St. Johns of to-day is a totally different place to the St. Johns of five years ago. The purifying element of fire a short time ago swept through the village. It had a good effect, causing the people to bestir themselves to clear away the debris and build anew. What is the consequence ? A fine, wide, main-street, lined on both sides with large and substantial brick buildings. These buildings are used for two purposes—shops beneath and rooms to let above. Whole families, if not too numerous, occupy flats, the entrance to which is through a door at the side of the shop, and thence by stairs to the different suites of rooms above. This arrangement is somewhat after the fashion of houses in Paris; a family on each flat, starting from the bottom to the top, with their names printed at the foot of the enormous flight of stairs.

That sort of thing has its draw-backs as well as

its advantages: the staircases are generally narrow, and the chances of running into collision with unknown people and dodging them on the stairs, not knowing which side to pass, is decidedly unpleasant; then, again, if the tap above is suffered to run through accident, a flood is the consequence, as water always endeavors to find its own level.

A stout old John Bull, who was desirous of visiting the capital of France before his visit to the next world, stood one day at the foot of one of the flights of stairs, endeavoring to make the Frenchman, who had just rented a flat to him understand that he expected to be taken up there by a hoist or, if possible, by some other means; "but walk up, decidedly out of the question, —absurd idea!"—"Vat is dat?" gesticulated the Frenchman. This sort of thing might have gone on *ad infinitum,* had not our friend happened to mention something about being raised; that word had certainly the good effect of bringing the futile talk of the two men, each using a different language for the interchange of thought to an end: for the Frenchman proceeded immediately to lead the excited English man a distance of several blocks to a hair-dresser where having deposited him in an easy-chair, requested the proprietor to lather his face preparatory to using the *razor.* The tableau vivant ends as might be expected under the circumstances: the old gentleman had no vocabulary equal to the occasion, and the Frenchman nearly subsided in total despair.

———

CHAPTER VIII.

THURSDAY MORNING, six o'clock.—Promise of another fine day. Bathed, that may be taken for granted in future, and consequently need not be mentioned again ; weighed anchor, and sailed through the draw-bridge, the last one homeward bound. We moored alongside a barge, having ascertained that it would remain there for the rest of the day. After breakfast, took a saunter ashore, met friends, and was introduced to the captain of the steamboat which was to take the next tow, now preparing for departure, to Montreal. Apart from his kind offer to tow us all the way home, he was a very nice fellow, and good company. We had several visitors down to see us : presently we heard the whistle of the steam-yacht signalling for the draw to open, and in a few minutes she steamed past us, looking gay and festive, with her bunting flying at both stem and stern.

After dining with a friend at the hotel we interviewed the chief, who said that he would get my clearance papers made out for me when he got his own, and that I had better make fast to his yacht, which we did accordingly. I had to go and tell the revenue officer that I regretted not having been informed of my duty to report myself, on my way to the lake, and that I hoped t was now all satisfactory. An answer in the affirmative terminated the interview.

At last we are off; steaming gaily down the twelve miles of canal that intervene between St. Johns and Chambly, but not going so fast as to exceed the regulation speed in canals, which is put down at so many knots an hour. We proceeded so smoothly that a blind man would not have known that he was moving at all unless told. The whistle was sounded as we approached every bridge and lock, as a signal to open for us. This mode of travelling is really most agreeable; we were all in high spirits, so exhilarating were the influences brought to bear on us, and the aspect of both land and water, and the circumstances of our agreeable mode of proceeding, presented a striking tableau. The last lock is passed; we have descended in safety what looks like a series of huge stone steps down to the basin of Chambly. What a contrast to our former experience in the canal on our way to the Lake! Now we felt peaceful and happy; then we were, or appeared to be, in the mood for anything from pitch and toss to manslaughter. Thus easily are weak mortals the playthings of circumstance. Tickle a man in the ribs, and he will laugh; hit him with a stick on the head, and the effect is different, if you are still alive to see the result of the experiment. The strong man is he who under all circumstances is the same : not elated by success nor dejected by failure.

> " Bless'd are those
> Whose blood and judgment are so well co-mingled,
> That they are not a pipe for fortune's finger
> To sound what stop she please."

But it is wonderful to think how susceptible we all are to outside influences. By far the majority of suicides have been committed upon dull rainy days, when

> " Mad from life's history,
> Glad to death's mystery," etc.

One could scarcely imagine any mortal on a bright cheerful day going out and hanging himself to the nearest tree. No; the grief which saps the mind is not alone sufficient to fill the black records of such crimes as these. Horrible expedient this ;— to rid oneself of the heavy responsibilities of life in the vain endeavor to rush into forgetfulness. The experiment is too dearly bought, I am afraid : nor can any man well afford to trifle with the vices which point the way to such tragedies.

But to continue, the steam yacht moored alongside the wharf, and we in turn alongside her. The ladies went ashore to the hotel, while the men wandered in various directions.

Later on in the evening I looked in upon some friends, and found that they were having a small dance; the consciousness that Johnny, the cabin-boy, was waiting for me on the beach caused me to leave early. I thought I would not put his fidelity to too great a test, or be answerable for the charge of cruelty to animals. On reaching the yacht, found the captain of the steam-tug boat with my friend : a counsel of war was held, which resulted in the unanimous decision that we would hook-on and be off, "no opportunity like the present," "strike while the iron is hot," etc. We might have to wait a long time for another tow to pass. The moon was full,—I do not mean to insinuate that the moon was not in a fit state,— and high in the heavens, as we noiselessly passed out into the middle of the basin, and towards the river. We established a watch, as one had to do some steering while passing Belœil bridge ; be-sides, it would have been very careless not to have one on the look-out.

The rising sun began to make himself felt from behind the airy curtains with which the river's mist enveloped us, while we like snails crawled out from our shells, and stretched our limbs. Presently there appeared breaks in the surround-ing mist, and land showed itself here and there, and presently everywhere. The locks of St. Ours were again reached, tea and milk procured, and on we went again. All the scenery was again passed in our downward course, and if possible appeared more beautiful than before. Finally Sorel was reached; we were saluted by a little shouting and waving of hats by a few on shore, which was returned with interest, especially by Johnny, who, feeling elated at the idea of being so near home, gave vent to his over-wrought feelings in the manner above described.

After we had rounded the sand-bar, and had fairly brested the current, it was not difficult to notice the slow rate of speed we were making; down to Sorel we had a slow current in our favor, stemming the current up from Sorel was "a horse of another color." We made the discovery that we were going at the rate of a mile and a quarter an hour, by observations made with reference to the time taken in passing certain objects on shore. The tow left Sorel, or passed it, as it did not stop there, at about mid-day on Friday, and was opposite Varennes at noon next day, Saturday, having accomplished thirty miles. I took the dingy, and rowed along the tow up to the steamboat. The way I managed to board the steamboat was by throwing a light halyard line, attached to the skiff, to a man on board, who pulled me alongside, above the paddle-wheels. One could not very well row up below the wheels, the commotion caused by them would disconcert a light skiff weighing only about sixty pounds.

" Well, Captain, the rate at which your boat is
going could not possibly justify the most sanguine
in thinking that we should make Longueuil before
another entire day has passed ! "   " Patience is a
virtue," he replied.

Soon after I had dropped down to the yacht,
we discerned a speck in the distance, which the
field-glass revealed to be the " Maud," the name
of our friend's steam-yacht.   She over-hauled us,
like an express train : salutes were exchanged, as
she flew along.   Presently, night closed around us,
as it did in ancient times around old Jacques
Cartier with his flotilla of canoes slowly paddling
up the river.   We ran the anchor light up to our
mast-head to prevent being run into by the Quebec
boat, which sometimes passes very close to the
stem of a tow in order to keep her channel.
The waves caused by that boat, coming thus suddenly, very nearly threw one of our crew over-
board by the unexpected rocking they gave to the
yacht.

Saturday, August 28.—The last day of our cruise
dawned upon us, struggling against the current, at
the foot of the island.   We fully expected to find
ourselves within sight of Montreal in the morning.
The steam engine, man's powerful servant, must
be at fault : there was a lamentable falling-off of
headway since last night.   Of course it was not a
matter of life and death, our reaching home that

day; but, as far as our inclinations were concerned, we were getting tired of that dead-and-alive
sort of thing, and preferred a little variety to break
the dull monotony of the snail-like progress.
Presently we stopped altogether, then our appre-
hensions began to take this form:—are we drift-
ing down; no, the steam boat had made fast to a
barge at anchor, and was at the same time working her engine at quarter speed. I found out
subsequently, that this was the time when the
captain went ashore and telegraphed for a steam
tug. Later on in the day we were delightfully
conscious that something new had happened to us,
as we were going through the water at a good
rate of speed. Our spirits went up with the increased speed, and our hope in better things was
not lessened by the fall of rain which was at the
time coming down heavily; the awning, together
with the cabin, kept us dry, and when the rain had
passed off we were well up the river at Long Point.

All tugs, with few exceptions, keep to the south
shore as they near Montreal and pass close to
Longueuil to avoid the current. However, to our
consternation and annoyance, the pilot kept in
mid-stream, which would leave us, when we cast
loose, opposite Longueuil, some distance out
in the current. If the prayers of the just availeth
much in this world, the maledictions of the un-
happy appeared as useless as the weeping over

crushed hopes and lost opportunities. There was
not a breath of wind, consequently we could not
sail out of the current and into our haven of rest.
On went the tow, and on we went ; we were now
opposite to Longueuil. Since we had no further
use of the tow we cast loose, and as we did so saw
a long flat-bottomed row-boat with eight men in
it. They, like the wise speculators of the world,
held aloof until the price for towing us in was
agreed upon ; the wise men would have got any
exorbitant figure they might have asked for, as we
were at their mercy. Two boarded us and got
out the sweeps, while a tow-line was thrown to
the men in the boat, and, finally, kind and indulgent
Reader, in this way we reached our moorings,
and the end of our cruise. The log-book was
closed and packed, it was the last article on board
left out, as we wished to give a true and faithful
cruise of the " Eurydice."

END.